Sunshine Daydreams

A Grateful Dead Journal

Sunshine Daydreams

A Grateful Dead
Journal

Herb Greene

Chronicle Books • San Francisco

"Grateful Dead Dancing Bears" are copyright © by
Grateful Dead Merchandising. "Grateful Dead Skeletons"
are copyright © by Grateful Dead Merchandising/artwork
by Rick Griffin. "Steal Your Face™" is a registered
trademark of Grateful Dead Merchandising, Inc.
"Grateful Dead" is a registered service mark of Grateful
Dead Productions, Inc.

Grateful Dead employee laminates and miscellaneous line
work are reproduced courtesy of Fine Line Design,.
copyright © 1991.

Lyrics from "U.S. Blues," "Wharf Rat," "Box of Rain,"
"Eyes of the World," "Dark Star," "Scarlet Begonias,"
"Candyman," "Friend of the Devil," and "Black Muddy
River," reprinted courtesy of Ice Nine Publishing
Company, Inc., copyright © Robert Hunter.

Lyrics from "I Need a Miracle," reprinted courtesy of Ice
Nine Publishing Company, Inc., copyright © by John
Barlow.

Album covers are copyright © by Grateful Dead
Productions, Inc.

Printed in Hong Kong.

ISBN 0-87701-813-8

Editing: Beth Haiken
Book and cover design: Ingalls + Associates, Inc.
Designer: Kendra Lawrence
Art Direction and Photography: Herb Greene

Editor's note: The dates in this book are accurate to the
best of our knowledge at press time. Several album
release dates can be dated by month and year only.

Distributed in Canada by Raincoast Books,
112 East Third Avenue, Vancouver, B.C. V5T 1C8

10 9 8 7 6 5 4 3 2 1

Chronicle Books
275 Fifth Street
San Francisco, CA 94103

This book is dedicated to
all you Dead Heads out there:
old and new, dudes and
dudettes, suited and tie-dyed.
Without you the Wheel would not
go round. I salute you.

Your pal,

Herb Greene

1967

"I need a woman 'bout twice my age
A lady of nobility, gentility, and rage,
A splendor in the dark, lightning on the draw,
We'll go right through the book
And break each and every law.
I got a feeling and it won't go away
Just one thing, then I'll be o.k.
I need a miracle everyday."

I Need a Miracle
John Barlow

1

"New Year's Day Wail," Panhandle, San Francisco, CA 1/1/67

Oakland, CA 1/1/91

2

NYC, NY 1/2/70

3

4

5

6

First Madison Square Garden show, NYC, NY 1/7/79

7

January

Bill Graham Presents

Grateful Dead

New Year's Eve

Monday
December 31, 1990
Oakland Coliseum Arena

7:00 pm Til It's Over
.00 General Adm

Nº 13166

Nº 13166

Grateful Dead
December 31, 1990
.00 General Admission

.00 Genera

Grateful Dead 1966

"When the last bolt of sunshine hits the mountain
And the stars start to splatter in the sky
When the moon splits the southwest horizon
With the scream of an eagle on the fly"

Black Muddy River
Robert Hunter

8

9

10 ⚡ Uniondale,
NY 1/10/79

11 ⚡ Chico, CA
1/11/68

12

13

14 "Great Human Be-In,"
Golden Gate Park,
San Francisco, CA
1/14/67

January

15

16

First Carousel
Ballroom (later
Fillmore West) show,
San Francisco, CA
1/17/68

17

 Corvallis, OR
1/17/70

18

19

 Eureka, CA
1/20/68

20

21

January

"Trips Festival,"
Longshoremens Hall,
San Francisco, CA
1/22/66 – 1/23/66

22

 Honolulu, HI
1/23/70

23

24

25

26

27 Wolfgang Mozart 1/27/1756

28

January

29

30

Warehouse, New
Orleans, LA. Band
gets busted following
gig. TC leaves.
1/30/70

31

DYLAN AND THE DEAD
1/31/89

 New Orleans,
LA 1/31/70

Dylan/Dead 1987

1

 St. Louis, MO
2/2/70

2

 Portland, OR
2/3/68

3

4

5

Bob Marley 2/6/1945

6

Last show at
Henry J. Kaiser
Convention Center,
Oakland, CA 2/7/89

7

Phil 1969

February

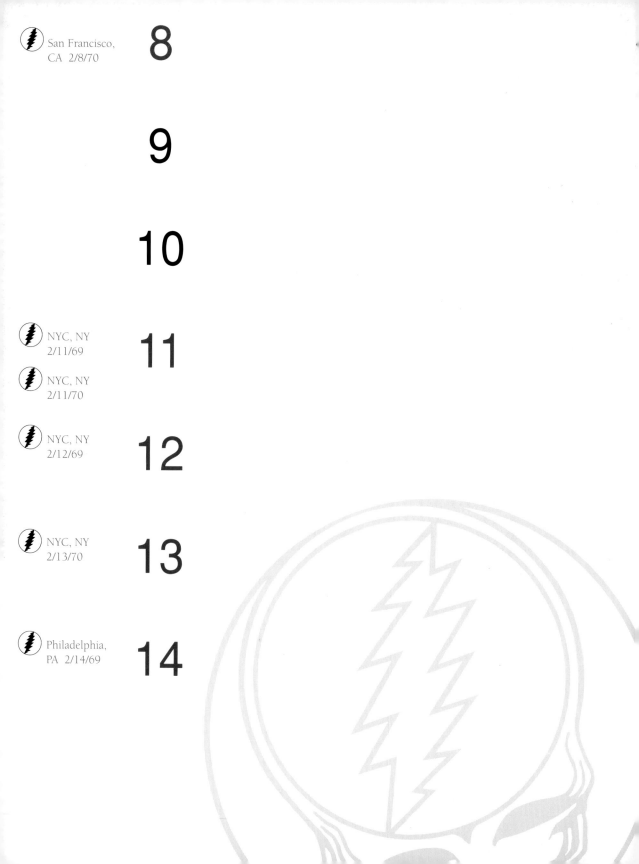

Grateful Dead 1979

February

Neal Cassady 1966

February

15  Philadelphia, PA 2/15/69

Madison, WI 2/15/73

16

17 Oakland Coliseum Arena "Rock for Life Benefit," Oakland, CA. Keith and Donna's last appearance with the band. 2/17/79

18 Capitol Theater, Port Chester, NY. Night of ESP experiment. Mickey leaves the band. 2/18/71

Port Chester, NY 2/18/71

19

20

Vince Welnick 2/21/1951 **21**

22

Vallejo, CA
2/22/69

Champaign -
Urbana, IL
2/22/73

23

24

Lake Tahoe,
CA 2/24/68

San Francisco,
CA 2/24/74

25

26

Lincoln, NB
2/26/73

27

San Francisco,
CA 2/27/69

28

San Francisco,
CA 2/28/69

February

1966/1990

SPRING 1989

ACCESS ALL AREAS

Laminate art by Tim Harris
Tie-dye by Not Fade Away Graphics

J. Garcia 1987

March

1  San Francisco,
CA   3/1/69

2  San Francisco,
CA   3/2/69

3 Free Show,
Haight Street,
San Francisco, CA
3/3/68

4

5

6

7

8

9

THE GRATEFUL DEAD
3/10/67

10

11

Bammies,
Civic Auditorium,
San Francisco, CA
3/12/88

12

13

14

March

Phil 1987

⚡ San Francisco,
CA 3/15/69

15 Phil Lesh 3/15/1940

⚡ San Francisco,
CA 3/16/68

⚡ Uniondale, NY
3/16/73

16

17

⚡ San Francisco,
CA 3/17/68

⚡ Buffalo, NY
3/17/70

18

19 Tom "TC" Constanten
3/19/1944

20

⚡ Utica, NY
3/21/73

21

March

22

Cow Palace, Daly City, CA. First "Wall of Sound" gig. 3/23/74

23

"Snack" benefit, Kezar Stadium, San Francisco, CA 3/23/75

NYC, NY 3/23/72

24

Dania, FL 3/24/70

Philadelphia, PA 3/24/73

25

Location unknown 3/26/68

26

Merced, CA 3/27/69

27

Essen, Germany, with The Who 3/28/81

Springfield, MA 3/28/73

28

Rhythym Devils 1987

29  Las Vegas, NV
3/29/69

Uniondale, NY
3/29/90

30

31

March

Bob 1979

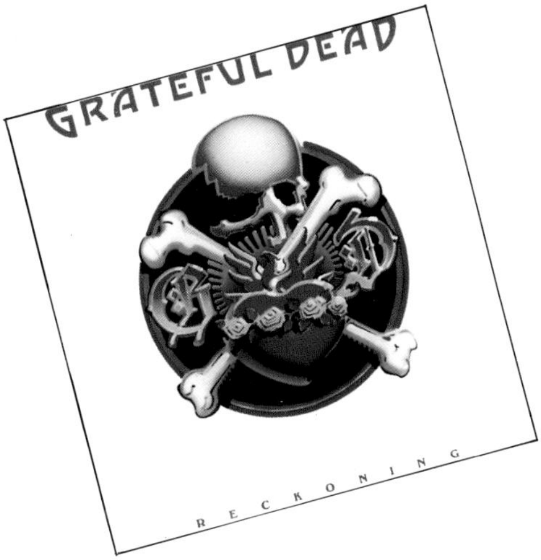

1 RECKONING
4/1/81

2

3

4 San Francisco,
CA 4/4/69

5 "Saturday Night Live."
Bobby wears bunny
ears. 4/5/80

San Francisco,
CA 4/5/69

6

7 Wembley Arena,
London. "Europe '72"
tour starts. 4/7/72

April

8

Boston, MA
4/8/71

Wembley,
England 4/8/72

9

10

San Francisco,
CA 4/11/70 **11**

12

Boulder, CO
4/13/69 **13**

Lewisburg, PA
4/14/71 **14**

Copenhagen,
Denmark
4/14/72

"Set out running but I take my time
A friend of the Devil is a friend of mine
If I get home before daylight
I might get some sleep tonight"

Friend of the Devil
Robert Hunter

April

Mickey 1967

Phil 1966

15

16

17　⚡ St. Louis, MO
4/17/69

⚡ Copenhagen,
Denmark
4/17/72

18

19

20

21　⚡ Boston, MA
4/21/69

April

Spartan Stadium, San Jose, CA. Brent's first show with the band. 4/22/79

22

 Boston, MA 4/22/69

 Boston, MA 4/23/69

23

 Denver, CO 4/24/70

24

 Dusseldorf, West Germany 4/24/72

 Denver, CO 4/25/70

25

 NYC, NY 4/26/71

26

 Minneapolis, MN 4/27/69

27

GO TO HEAVEN 4/28/80

28

 NYC, NY 4/28/71

April

Duke Ellington 4/29/1899

29

Last Fillmore East
performance, NYC,
NY 4/29/71

 Hamburg,
West Germany
4/29/72

30

The Warlocks 1965

"Walk out of any doorway
feel your way, feel your way
like the day before
Maybe you'll find direction
around some corner
where it is waiting to meet you—"

Box of Rain
Robert Hunter

May

1

2

3 Columbia University
during student strike,
NYC, NY 5/3/68

 San Francisco,
CA 5/3/69

4 Paris, France
5/4/72

5 Central Park, NYC,
NY 5/5/68

6 Outdoors at M.I.T.,
Cambridge, MA,
during student strike
in protest of Kent
State killings 5/6/70

Polo Field, Golden
Gate Park, San
Francisco, CA 5/7/69

Johannes Brahms 5/7/1833
Billy Kreutzman 5/7/1946

7 Last performance at
Frost Amphitheater,
Stanford University,
Palo Alto, CA 5/7/89

 San Francisco,
CA 5/7/69

 Manchester,
England
5/7/72

WORKINGMAN'S DEAD
5/70

8

First show at Laguna
Seca Raceway,
Monterey, CA 5/9/87

9

Pasadena, CA
5/10/69

10

Rotterdam,
The Netherlands
5/11/72

11

12

13

Missoula, MT
5/14/74

14

May

Jerry 1970

"Once in a while
you get shown the light
in the strangest of places
if you look at it right."

Scarlet Begonias
Robert Hunter

15 NYC, NY
5/15/70

16

17

18 "Northern California
Folk-Rock Festival,"
Santa Clara, CA
5/18/68

 Munich,
West Germany
5/18/72

19 First show at Avalon
Ballroom,
San Francisco, CA
5/19/66

20

21

May

22

 London,
England
5/23/72

23

"Hollywood
Festivals," Newcastle-
Under-Lyme,
England. First
appearance overseas.
5/24/70

24

 Newcastle-
Under-Lyme,
England
5/24/70

 London,
England
5/25/72

25

Strand Lyceum,
London, England.
"Europe '72" tour
ends. 5/26/72

26

27

Vietnam Veterans'
benefit, Moscone
Center, San Francisco,
CA 5/28/82

28

May

29 HISTORIC DEAD
5/71

30 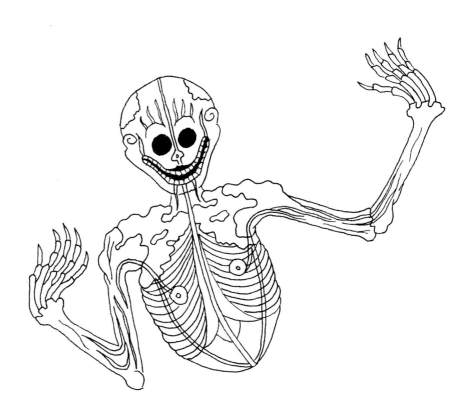 Portland, OR
5/30/69

31

GRATEFUL·DEAD

1989

SUMMER

ACCESS ALL AREAS

Laminate art by Tim Harris
Tie-dye by Not Fade Away Graphics

Tompkins Square
Park, NYC, NY. First
New York appearance.
6/1/67

1

Billy 1967

2

Paramount Theater,
Portland, OR. The
Dead resume touring.
6/3/76

3

4

5

6

"Fifteenth
Anniversary
Celebration," Folsom
Field, Boulder, CO
6/7/80 – 6/8/80

7

 San Francisco,
CA 6/7/68

June

Vince Welnick 1991

June

8

9 First performance at Cal. Expo. Amphitheater, Sacramento, CA 6/9/84

10 Washington, DC 6/10/73

11

12

13

14 First Fillmore East performance, NYC, NY 6/14/68

20th Anniversary Show, Greek Theater, Berkeley, CA. "Sgt. Pepper's" is played before show at full volume, rendering much of P.A. system useless. 6/14/85

 Monterey, CA 6/14/69

15

16

17 Hollywood Bowl, Hollywood, CA. Pigpen's last performance. 6/17/72

18 Phil's first gig. Frenchy's, Hayward, CA. 6/18/65

Monterey Pop Festival, Monterey, CA 6/18/67

19 Anchorage, AK 6/19/80 – 6/21.80

20 AOXOMOXOA 6/20/69

21 Chateau D'Herouville, Herouville, France. First performance on European mainland. 6/21/80

June

Central Park, NYC,
NY 6/22/69

22

NYC, NY
6/22/69

Miami, FL
6/23/74

23

Port Chester,
NY 6/24/70

24

25

STEAL YOUR FACE
6/26/76

26

MARS HOTEL
6/27/74

27

Santa Rosa, CA
6/27/69

First appearance at
Oakland Auditorium
(later Henry J. Kaiser
Convention Center),
Oakland, CA 6/28/67

28

June

(sic)

GRATEFUL DEAD FROM THE MARS HOTEL

Universal City,
CA 6/30/73

Jerry 1967

Captain Trips 1966

"Wave that flag
Wave it wide and high
Summertime done come and gone
My, oh, my
Summertime done come and gone
My, oh, my"

U.S. Blues
Robert Hunter

1

2 Last appearance at
Fillmore West,
San Francisco, CA
7/2/71

3

4 First "Dylan and The
Dead" gig. Foxboro,
MA 7/4/87

5

6 IN THE DARK
7/6/87

7 First show at Red
Rocks Amphitheater,
Morrison, CO 7/7/78

July

8

9

10

11

12

13

14

Bob Weir 1986

July

15

16

First show in
Ventura, CA 7/17/82

17

ANTHEM OF THE SUN
7/18/68

 Jersey City, NJ
7/18/72

18

19

Keith Godchaux
7/19/1948

20

21

July

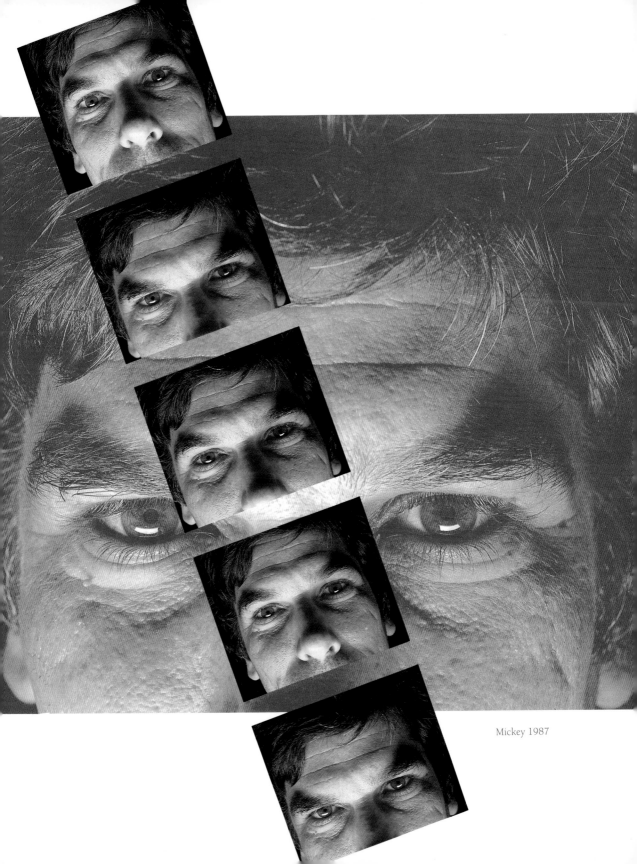

Mickey 1987

22

23

24

Chicago, IL
7/25/74

25

26

Watkins Glen, NY
7/27/73 – 7/28/73

TERRAPIN STATION
7/27/77

27

28

July

29 Vancouver, BC. First
show outside of U.S.
7/29/66

30

31 Last show at Laguna
Seca Raceway,
Monterey, CA
7/31/88

New Haven,
CT 7/31/71

Bob,

Brent,

Bill,

and Phil 1987

"Wake up to find out
that you are the eyes of the world"

Eyes of the World
Robert Hunter

Jerry Garcia 8/1/1942

1

2

3

4

5

6

7

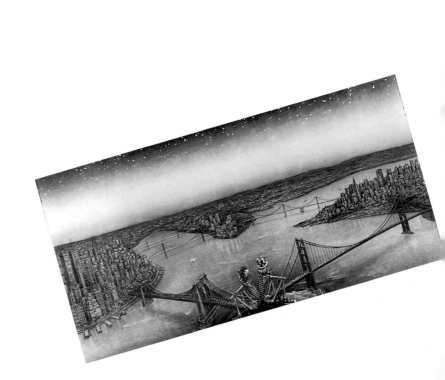

J. Garcia 1966

August

8

9

10

11

12

13

14

"... 'cause I know that the life I'm
living's no good
I'll get a new start
and live the life I should
I'll get up and fly away ..."

Wharf Rat
Robert Hunter

August

Pig 1969

Mickey and Billy 1969

August

15

16 Woodstock, NY
8/16/69

17

18

19 Last show at Greek
Theater, Berkeley, CA
8/19/89

20  San Francisco,
CA 8/20/68

21 San Francisco,
CA 8/21/68

 Berkeley, CA
8/21/72

22

San Francisco, CA 8/22/68

Donna Godchaux 8/22/1947

23

First show at Alpine Valley Music Theater, East Troy, WI 8/23/80

Los Angeles, CA 8/23/68

24

Los Angeles, CA 8/24/68

25

26

27

Springfield Creamery benefit, Veneta, OR 8/27/72

Veneta, OR 8/27/72

28

Springfield Creamery presents "Second Decadenal Field Trip," Veneta, OR 8/28/82

San Francisco, CA 8/28/68

August

Jerry 1969

GRATEFUL DEAD

Fall
1989
Winter

Laminate art by Tim Harris
Tie-dye by Joyce Kuchar

1

2

3

4

5

6

7

Grateful Dead 1966

September

Mountain Girl and Garcia

September

Ron "Pigpen" McKernan
9/8/1945

8

London, England.
"Europe '74" tour
starts. 9/9/74

9

 Hollywood,
CA 9/10/72

10

 London,
England
9/10/74

Mickey Hart 9/11/1943

11

Williamsburg,
VA 9/11/73

12

13

Cairo, Egypt
9/14/78 – 9/16/78

14

15

16 (⚡) Boston, MA
9/16/72

17 (⚡) NYC, NY
9/17/70

18

19 (⚡) NYC, NY
9/19/70

20 (⚡) NYC, NY
9/20/90

21 Paris, France.
"Europe '74" tour
ends. 9/21/74

(⚡) Philadelphia,
PA 9/21/72

September

22

23

Rainforest benefit,
Madison Square
Garden, NYC, NY
9/24/88

24

 Waterbury, CT
9/24/72

The Dead start a
fifteen night run at
the Warfield Theater,
San Francisco, CA.
They revive acoustic
sets. 9/25/80

25

26

 Jersey City, NJ
9/27/72

27

Lindley Meadows in
Golden Gate Park,
San Francisco, CA
9/28/75

28

September

29 Straight Theater, San Francisco, CA. Mickey joins the band. 9/29/67

30 Edinburgh, Scotland. "Europe '81" tour starts. 9/30/81

Grateful Dead 1967

First show at Greek
Theater, Berkeley, CA
10/1/67

1

First gig at Shoreline
Amphitheater,
Mountain View, CA.
The 20th anniversary
of 710 Ashbury
bust. They play
"Truckin." 10/2/87

2

3

Winterland, the night
Janis Joplin dies
10/4/70

4

5

"Lunatic Protest
Demonstration,"
Panhandle,
San Francisco, CA.
LSD becomes illegal
in California. 10/6/66

6

First performance at
Winterland,
San Francisco, CA
10/7/66

7

October

VINTAGE DEAD
10/70

8

"Dead Roadies'
Benefit," Winterland,
San Francisco, CA
10/9/72

9

First show at Frost
Amphitheater,
Stanford University,
Palo Alto, CA
10/9/82

 San Francisco,
CA 10/9/68

10

 Hampton, VA
10/9/89

Oakland Stadium
with The Who,
Oakland, CA
10/9/72 – 10/10/72

11

 San Francisco,
CA 10/10/68

 Paterson, NJ
10/11/70

12

 San Francisco,
CA 10/13/68

13

14

October

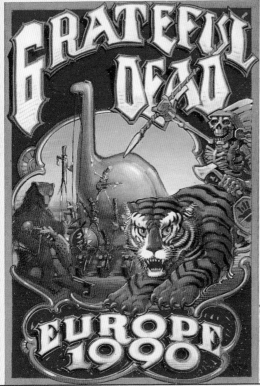

GRATEFUL DEAD

EUROPE 1990

Montag, 22. Oktober 1990 · 20.00 Uhr

FRANKFURT · FESTHALLE

Vorverkauf: DM 40,–
zuzügl. Vorverkaufsgebühr, inkl. 7 % MwSt.,
zuzüglich DM 1,– für die Leistungen des FVV.

Abendkasse: DM 46,–
inkl. 7 % MwSt.

KEIN SITZPLATZANSPRUCH!

FVV-Ticket für die Hin- und Rückfahrt. Gültig auf allen FVV-Linien für 1 Fahrt in der 2. Klasse zur Festhalle Frankfurt und zurück. Hinfahrt frühestens 3 Stunden vor Veranstaltungsbeginn; Rückfahrt bis Betriebsschluß am Veranstaltungstag. Es gelten die Gemeinsamen Beförderungsbedingungen und Tarifbestimmungen. (Benutzung der 1. Wagenklasse S-Bahn nur mit Zuschlag).

№ 93

Wichtiger Hinweis siehe Rückseite!

Kontroll-Abriß

№ 93

№ Kontroll-Abriß
2786

Grateful Dead 1969

15 WAKE OF THE FLOOD 10/15/73

Bob Weir 10/16/1947

16 Last bar gigs, Club Melk-Weg, Amsterdam, The Netherlands 10/15/81 – 10/16/81

 East Rutherford, NJ 10/16/89

17

18  St. Louis, MO 10/18/72

San Francisco, CA 10/18/74

Minneapolis, MN. Keith joins the band. 10/19/71

19 Barcelona, Spain. "Europe '81" tour ends. 10/19/81

San Francisco, CA 10/19/68

20 Oklahoma City, OK 10/19/73

The Dead stop touring, pack in "Wall of Sound." Mickey returns. 10/20/74

Dizzy Gillespie 10/21/1917
Brent Mydland 10/21/1952

21 Berlin, Germany 10/20/90

 Chicago, IL 10/21/71

October

22

23

24

San Francisco, CA 10/25/69

Indianapolis, IN 10/25/73

25

Miami, FL 10/26/89

26

27

Cleveland, OH 10/28/72

28

October

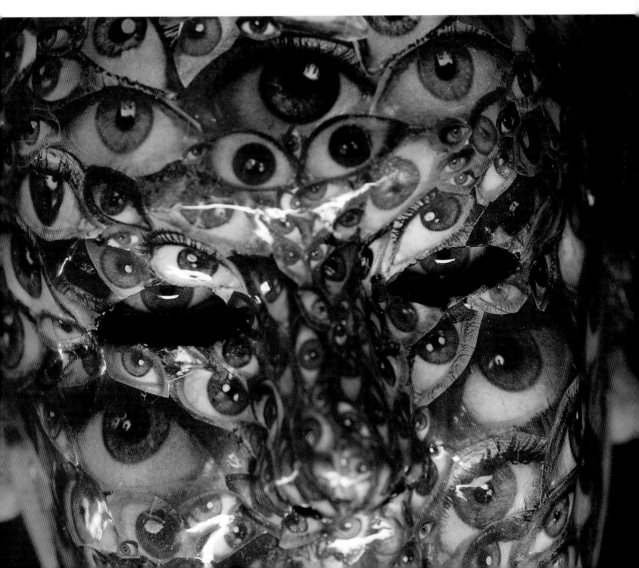
In the Dark 1987

AMERICAN BEAUTY
11/70

London,
England
11/1/90

1

2

3

4

Port Chester,
NY 11/5/70

5

6

San Francisco,
CA 11/7/69

San Francisco,
CA 11/7/71

7

Bobby 1969

November

San Francisco,
CA 11/8/69

Port Chester,
NY 11/8/70

8

9

LIVE DEAD
11/10/69

10

First appearance on
"Saturday Night Live."
Phil wears a large
"Hi Mom" button.
11/11/78

11

12   Neil Young 11/12/1945

13

14

"Shall we go,
you and I
while we can?
Through
the transitive nightfall
of diamonds?"

Dark Star
Robert Hunter

November

Garcia 1987

November

15   SHAKEDOWN STREET
11/15/78

EUROPE '72
11/72

 Austin, TX
11/15/71

16

17

18

19    Houston, TX
11/19/72

20

21

Billy 1979

22

Tom Constanten joins
The Dead in Athens,
OH 11/23/68

23

24

Bruce Hornsby 11/25/1955

25

 San Antonio,
TX 11/26/72

26

27

28

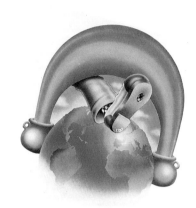

November

J. Garcia 1969

FALL
WINTER
TOUR

GRATEFUL DEAD 1988

ACCESS ALL AREAS

Laminate art by Tim Harris
Tie-die by Not Fade Away Graphics

Grateful Dead 1968

December

1

2

3

4  San Francisco,
CA 12/4/69

5 NYC, NY
12/5/71

6 Cleveland, OH
12/6/73

7

GRATEFUL DEAD

Billy and Pig 1966

December

8

9

10

San Francisco Mime
Troupe benefit. First
performance at
Fillmore Auditorium,
San Francisco, CA
12/10/65

Los Angeles,
CA 12/10/69

11

Los Angeles,
CA 12/11/69

San Francisco,
CA 12/11/72

12

Denver, CO
12/12/90

13

Los Angeles,
CA 12/13/67

14

Denver, CO
12/14/90

©G.D.M.,inc.

Oakland Coliseum,
Oakland, CA. First
show since Garcia's
recuperation.
12/15/86

15

 Long Beach,
CA 12/15/72

16

17

Tampa, FL
12/18/73

18

19

San Francisco,
CA 12/20/69

20

21

December

Grateful Dead 1968

22

23

24

25

26

27

28

December

29

30 Boston, MA
12/30/69

31 Donna's first
performance with The
Dead. Winterland,
San Francisco, CA
12/31/71

The Grateful Dead
close Winterland, San
Francisco, CA
12/31/78

BUILT TO LAST
12/31/89

 San Francisco,
CA 12/31/68

 San Francisco,
CA 12/31/78

 Oakland, CA
12/31/81

 Oakland, CA
12/31/89

 Oakland, CA
12/31/90

Notes

Notes

Notes

J. Garcia 1990

"Hand me my old guitar
Pass the whiskey 'round
Want you to tell everybody you meet
the Candyman's in town."

Candyman
Robert Hunter

Because a project like this takes the help and cooperation of many people, I would like to mention as many of them as possible.

My first thanks go to the people who helped me get started with this project: Robert Hunter for writing truly great lyrics that make listening to the Dead compelling; my good friend and cosmic consultant, Nancy "Willie" Wilson for showing me a "really" good time at many shows over the years; Anne Carey for her ticket stubs and for giving me a new and appreciative perspective on the wonderful world of "Dead Heads"; because he is always there, David Gans; and David Barich, Karen Pike, Lisa Howard, and Nion McEvoy at Chronicle Books. And the winners for excellence in design are Tom Ingalls and Kendra Lawrence.

The materials and information in this book were collected from many dedicated supporters. The guys at Dead Base, John W. Scott, Stu Nixon, and especially Mike Dolgushkin, provided a wealth of data. Steve Marcus and Frankie Accardi of the Grateful Dead ticket office gave me access to their personal collections. Tim Harris provided access to his rare collection of fantastic laminate designs. Martin Leffer, of Not Fade Away Graphics, provided some of the tie-dyes. The fine photographic printing was done by David and Cissy Spindler (black and white) of Spindler photographics and David Peterson (color) of Faulkner Color Lab.

Thanks also for the cooperation and contributions of Calico, Bill Belmont, Patricia Harris, Blair Jackson, Jon McIntire, Dennis McNally, Danny Rifkin, Cameron Sears, Tony Secunda, Jan Simmons, Sue Swanson, Robbie Taylor, and Brian Kemble.

The entire Grateful Dead organization has been terrifically supportive, but most of all I'd like to thank the ladies in the office for their continual help. Eileen Law has been particularly helpful, along with Annette Flowers, Diane Geoppo, Janet Knudsen, Cassidy Law, Nancy Mallonee, Mary Jo Meinolf, Maruska Nelson, Basia Raizene, Jeanni Rasmussen, and Sue Stephens.

Of course, no thank you list would be complete without mentioning the intrepid crew: Bill Candelario, John Cutler, Billy Grillo, Bill Langevin, Steve Parish, Harry Popick, Bob Bralove, and most of all "Ram Rod" Shurtliff for his steadfast friendship.

Expect a miracle,

Herb Greene